8 original pieces for the late intermediate to early advanced pianist

MARTHA MIER

Jazz is an important and distinctive American contribution to 20th-century music. *Jazz, Rags and Blues, Book 5*, contains eight original solos that reflect the various styles of the jazz idiom. From the bright and happy sound of "Opening Night Jazz" to the slow blues swing style of "Blue Interlude," students will love the challenge of playing in the jazz style.

Jazz is fun to play! Students will be inspired and motivated by the syncopated rhythms and the colorful, rich harmonies of jazz—a style that has captured the imagination of performer and listener alike!

Alfred

Copyright © MMIX by Alfred Music
ISBN-10: 0-7390-6051-1
ISBN-13: 978-0-7390-6051-3

Opening Night Jazz

Martha Mier

4

for Julia Catherine Yarbrough

Memphis Blues

Martha Mier

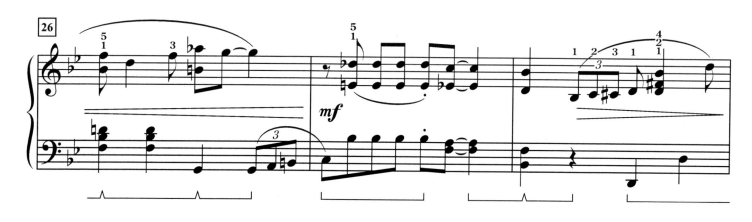

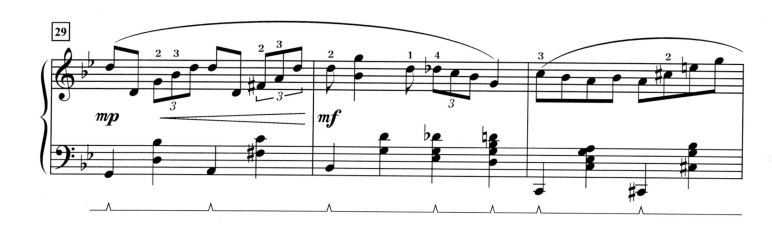

for Leighton Murri

HOT POTATO RAG

Martha Mier

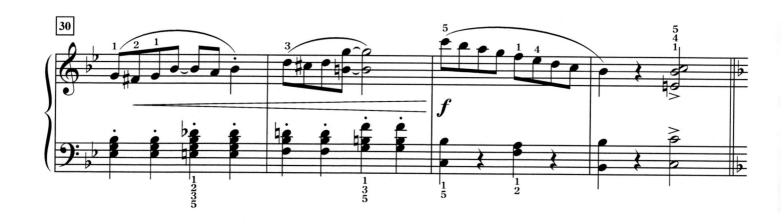

Steamboat Jazz

Martha Mier

River City Blues

Martha Mier

PERSNICKETY RAG

Martha Mier

Evenly, with a steady beat (Play ♪♪ evenly)

Blue Interlude

Martha Mier

Jazz Finale

Martha Mier

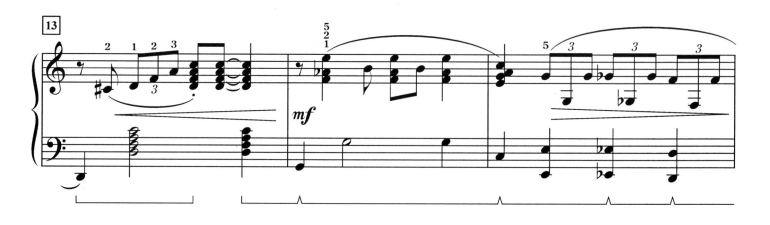

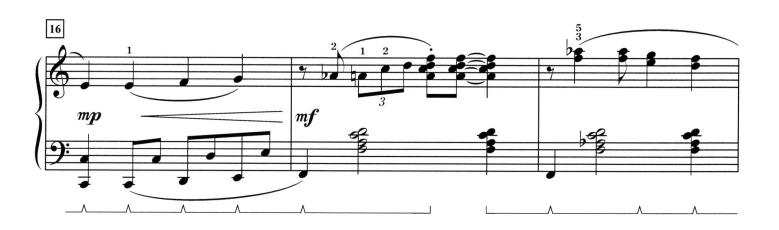

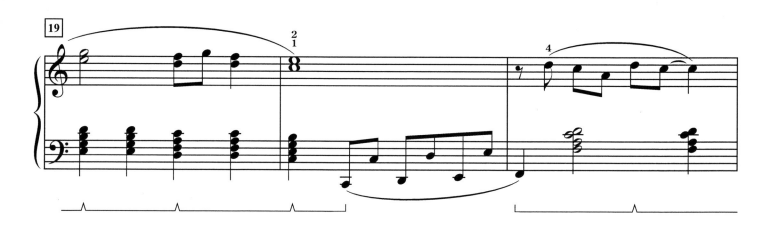

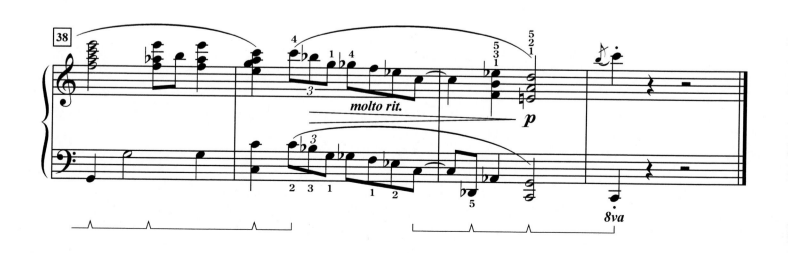